Where Is
the Parthenon?

by Roberta Edwards

illustrated by John Hinderliter

Penguin Workshop

For Ruby, who wants to make her own book—JH

PENGUIN WORKSHOP
An imprint of Penguin Random House LLC, New York

First published in the United States of America by Penguin Workshop,
an imprint of Penguin Random House LLC, New York, 2016

Text copyright © 2016 by Roberta Edwards
Illustrations copyright © 2016 by Penguin Random House LLC

Visit us online at penguinrandomhouse.com.

Library of Congress Control Number: 2015040449

Printed in the United States of America

ISBN 9780448488899   10 9 8 7

Contents

Where Is the Parthenon?

Imagine going back in time 2,500 years to the city of Athens in ancient Greece. It is just about sunrise. You and your parents leave your small mud-brick house and join a large parade of people climbing up a steep hill that rises from the center of the city. Men and women—as well as you and the other young children—are wearing capes over loose, white tunics called *chitons* (say: ky-tuns). Wearing light clothing helps everyone stay cool in the heat of the sun.

Where is everyone going?

They are heading to a temple that stands on top of the hill. It is made of white marble with a ring of forty columns going around all four sides. It is called the Parthenon (say: PAR-thuh-nahn). Everyone has come here to worship the goddess Athena. The Parthenon is the goddess's special temple.

Superhumans

The ancient Greeks worshipped many gods and goddesses. But Athena, the goddess of wisdom and war, was the favorite of the people of Athens. She protected their city. Athens was named for her. Her father, Zeus, was king of the gods. He controlled thunder and lightning. His wife was Hera. Zeus was not always faithful to her, which made Hera really mad. One of Zeus's brothers, Poseidon, was king of the seas, and another, named Hades, ruled over the dead. According to legend, all the gods and goddesses lived on Olympus, the highest mountain in Greece. The gods were not all that different from human beings—except that they were bigger, more beautiful, and way more powerful.

Hera

Zeus

Apollo

Ares

Poseidon

Hades

Athena

Your family follows the parade to the front of the Parthenon. The temple is decorated with brightly painted sculptures made by the most famous artists. The outside of the temple is grand and beautiful. Still, it does not compare with what you will see inside.

You and your family pass through the columns and enter a dark room. You gaze up. Towering above you is a statue of mighty Athena. The "skin" on her face is made of ivory, and her robes are covered in sheets of real gold—more than two thousand pounds of it. The goddess of war is dressed for battle. She wears a helmet, and armor over her chest. With her shield and spear, she is ready to fight against the enemies of Athens. She is a giant. She is almost forty feet tall! What harm can possibly come to your city when mighty Athena is protecting it?

Now jump ahead to modern times. You are in Athens again, on the same sunny hilltop, standing among a crowd of people snapping photos in front of the same temple.

What do you see now?

Actually, it is easier to list all the things you *don't* see. The paint on the temple is gone. The roof is gone. So are many of the columns and most of the sculptures on the outside of the temple. As for the giant statue of Athena, there is no trace of it or the room in which the statue stood.

For hundreds of years the Parthenon has been in ruins. Still, it remains one of the most famous places in the world. As famous as the Great Pyramids of Egypt and the Great Wall of China.

The Great Pyramids

The three huge pyramids outside Cairo are far older than the Parthenon. They were built by the rulers, called *pharaohs*, of ancient Egypt more than 4,500 years ago.

The Great Wall of China

The Great Wall stretches for more than four thousand miles (though it was originally much longer) and was built to protect the ancient empire of China. Construction on the first part of the Great Wall began about two hundred years before the Parthenon.

In the case of the Parthenon, it is not size that makes it so special. It is because of its beauty. Each year, throngs of tourists climb up the hill and, under the blazing Greek sun, walk around the remains of the temple. Even as a ruin, it is unforgettable.

So what happened to the Parthenon? Why was this world-famous landmark almost destroyed? And who was to blame?

Greece Today

Today, Greece is a modern nation in southern Europe that includes many islands in the Aegean Sea. The whole population is under twelve million people. (That's about the same as the state of Ohio.) The land is very mountainous, and not much of it is good for farming. (The major product is olive oil; it comes from olive trees, which have been grown there since ancient times.) The summers in Greece are hot and dry, and it usually rains only in winter. Athens, where the Parthenon stands, is the capital and the largest city. About 665,000 people live there.

CHAPTER 1
A Golden Moment, a Golden Leader

In the long history of the world, certain moments stand out because of all the new and exciting things taking place. In Athens, Greece, the middle of the fifth century BC—that's about 450 years before Jesus was born—counts as one of those special times. It didn't last very long—only eighteen years. However, it's still remarkable that so many incredible things happened then.

The way that people were ruled changed. For the very first time, ordinary people—not kings or lords, and not just rich people—got to have power and govern themselves. They could decide what laws they wanted to live by. These ordinary people were known as the *demos*, and our kind of government, democracy, comes from that Greek word. *Democracy* means a government that is controlled by the people.

It was a time of peace when the arts flourished. Beautiful plays—funny ones as well as sad ones—were written during this golden time. Some of these plays are still performed today in theaters all around the world. And some of the greatest sculptors left their mark on the city of Athens on a hill called the Acropolis.

At the very center of this golden age was a man named Pericles (say: PEH-ruh-kleez). In fact, this period of time is sometimes called the Age of Pericles.

Pericles of Athens was born in 495 BC. His father was a powerful soldier and politician. His mother came from an important family. Pericles grew up loving art and science. He held the position of *strategos* (say: strat-ay-gos) for nearly thirty years. A *strategos* was a general. But really, Pericles was much more than a high-ranking soldier. He was the leader of Athens.

Pericles believed that it was every person's duty to take part in government and in the life of the city. For instance, he thought all people should serve on juries. Not just the rich. Poor people, however, couldn't afford to take off from work to be jurors on trials, even if the trial was a short one. So Pericles came up with the idea of paying people for jury time. Today, in the United States, people are paid to serve on juries.

Pericles in full armor

Democracy—Sort Of

In ancient Athens, for the first time in history, people were allowed to elect leaders. They also could vote on laws and on issues such as whether to start wars. But "people" did not mean "everybody." Only men who were born in Athens had these rights. Women couldn't vote. Neither could foreigners or slaves.

The ruling body was known as the assembly. It was a gathering of all voters and met outdoors at a hill west of the Acropolis. Six thousand people had to be present in the assembly before a vote could be taken to pass a law. More important than the ordinary citizens in the assembly was a group of about five hundred leaders called the council. At the very top were ten military leaders also in charge of the city. They could be reelected over and over.

Pericles stayed in power for almost all of his adult life, about thirty years.

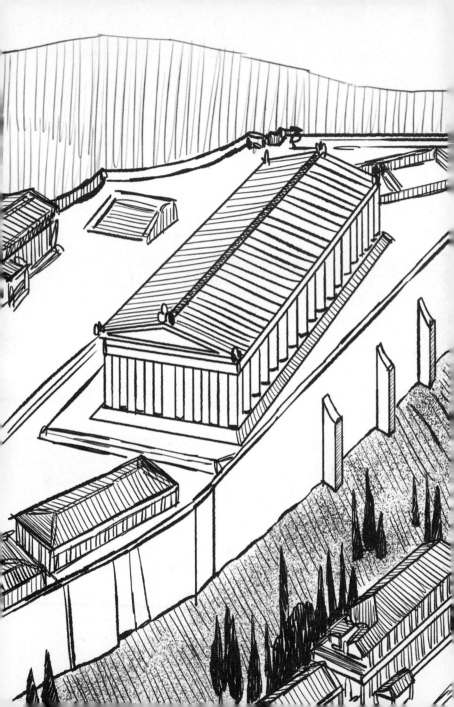

Pericles believed that the arts weren't just for entertainment. He thought that they actually made people smarter and better. That's why he wanted everyone to see the plays of Sophocles and Euripedes and Aristophanes. Because going to plays was expensive, Pericles saw to it that free tickets were given to the poor. He had a huge open-air theater built below the Acropolis that could seat thousands of people.

Pericles's goal was to make Athens the most glorious city in all of Greece. According to an ancient writer, Pericles said that the people of Athens were "lovers of the beautiful, yet simple in our tastes . . . we do not copy our neighbors but are an example to them." Pericles was saying that the people of Athens were special. They did not copy others; others copied them.

At the time, Greece was not a country. The area it now occupies was a scattering of about a hundred cities that each ruled itself. Athens had become the most powerful of them. During Pericles's lifetime, the cities all banded together and put up lots of money to build a large fleet of ships. A strong navy would protect them against their archenemy—the Persians.

Pericles, however, wanted to use a lot of the money for gorgeous new buildings in Athens. The other cities didn't like that idea one bit. Why should their money go to make Athens look so grand?

Sea-Onion Head

There are many images of Pericles from ancient times—in statues and on coins, for example. In every single one, he is shown wearing a helmet. He was a general, and so picturing him in a helmet doesn't seem unusual. However, the historian Plutarch said there was another reason for the headgear. Pericles's head was extra-big, and wearing a helmet helped to hide that fact. Comics in ancient Athens teased Pericles about his big noggin. In fact, his nickname was "sea-onion head," after a bulbous plant that grew on the coast.

Even in Athens, some people were against the building projects. They complained that Pericles "was gilding their city and ornamenting it with statues and costly temples as a proud and vain woman decks herself out in jewels."

Pericles was a proud and stubborn man. He rarely appeared in public and didn't like most people. In fact, it was said that, in his whole life, he never once had dinner with a friend. But he was a very gifted orator. That means he could persuade people with his words. In speeches, he was able to convince the assembly—the ruling body in Athens—to let him go ahead with his plan. Even so, the assembly made sure that Pericles kept the workers on schedule and, just as important, that he never spent more than what the assembly had okayed. If he needed more money, he had to go and ask for it.

It made sense to choose the Acropolis—a hilltop that rose five hundred feet above the city—as the spot to build on. It had always been looked upon as a sacred site, a place to worship the gods. Temples had been there for centuries. Also, because the Acropolis was the highest point in Athens, buildings on it could be seen from anywhere in the city.

Pericles's plan was to erect not just one but three temples up there, as well as a grand gateway leading to them. The work got underway in 447 BC. Amazingly, in just fifteen years, the biggest building, the Parthenon, was finished! (By comparison, the famous cathedral of Notre-Dame in Paris was started in 1163 . . . almost fifteen hundred years later. It took almost two hundred years to finish.)

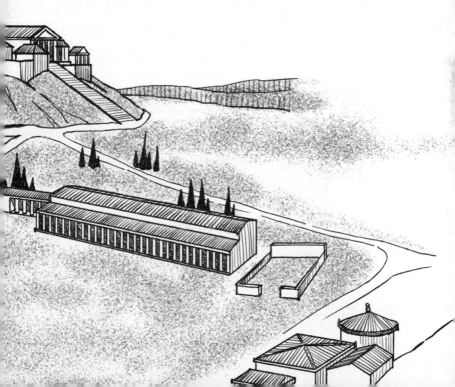

Outdoor Worship

Today, people enter the inside of churches and synagogues and mosques to worship and pray. This was not the case in ancient Greece. Although there were priests and priestesses at the temples, no services were held inside. The temple was considered the home of a god or goddess. So people stood outside and offered their prayers. Sacrifices of animals—often cows—were also offered to the gods on an altar outside the temple. Every temple was devoted to one particular god: to Zeus, to Poseidon, or—as in the case of the Parthenon—to Athena.

CHAPTER 2
Partners

Pericles knew exactly who were the best people to carry out his great project. Fortunately, the assembly approved all of his choices. The architect was Iktinos (say: ick-TIE-ness). He was going to design the temple. He did not work from detailed plans like architects do today. He probably just used rough drawings. His top assistant was another architect named Kallikrates (say: cal-uh-KRAY-tees). He was in charge of the workers.

The sculptor Phidias

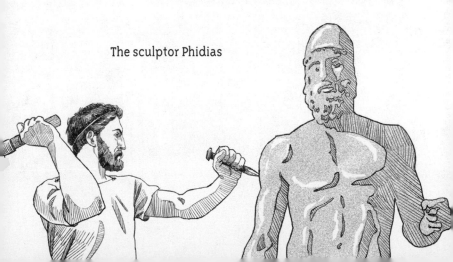

The most famous sculptor of the day was going to make the statue of the goddess Athena and design the rest of the sculptures. His name was Phidias (say: fiddy-iss). Phidias was a very good friend of Pericles. The two men worked together very closely on all plans for the Parthenon.

Planned as the biggest temple in all of Greece, the Parthenon was going to be near the ruins of an older temple. The exact spot was the very highest point of the Acropolis. Years earlier, the Persians had invaded Athens and destroyed everything in the city and on the Acropolis. The ruins of the older temple were left as they were.

This was to make sure no one in Athens would ever forget the terrible attack. To this day, you can still see pieces of columns from the older temple in the wall of the Acropolis.

Job, Jobs, and More Jobs

Not only would the new temples on the Acropolis prove the power and glory of Athens—building them provided lots of jobs. The people of Athens were very happy about that. Stonemasons, sculptors, and painters were needed. So were workers to do less skilled jobs, such as making carts to carry building supplies, weaving ropes to secure supplies on the carts, and building roads along which the carts could travel. A lot of slave labor was probably used for the toughest jobs, such as loading and unloading marble blocks. Slaves were often enemy soldiers who had been taken prisoner in past wars. Possibly as many as twenty thousand people were involved with the work on the Parthenon.

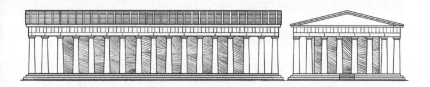

Using geometric shapes like rectangles and triangles, the design for the Parthenon was very simple and yet very pleasing to the eye. It is a symmetrical—or balanced—building. Its front and back mirror each other. So do the sides. Basically, the Parthenon is a rectangular box with columns going around all four sides. It is a simple post-and-lintel construction. The columns are the posts. They hold up crosswise beams—the lintels. On the Parthenon, the lintels support a sloping roof.

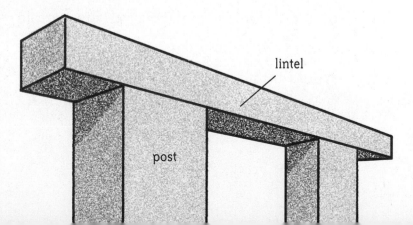

lintel

post

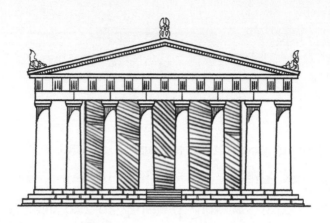

The plan called for eight outer columns across the front and back. That was two more than on most temples. Along the sides were seventeen outer columns. That was more than usual, too. The base of the temple measures 228 feet by 101.4 feet. The temple needed to be bigger than average to provide enough space for the giant statue of Athena that was going to stand in an inner room. A sloping roof covered the temple and provided two triangular spaces where large statues would be placed. Even without *blueprints* (detailed drawings of the building's plan), the work was carried out very precisely.

Was the Parthenon the Largest Temple in Ancient Greece?

For a while it was. But then the title of biggest went to a temple to Zeus, also in the city of Athens, not far from the Acropolis. Today, all that remains of it are some gigantic columns—each almost fifty-six feet high. Work actually began a century before the Parthenon was built, but the temple to Zeus wasn't finished until AD 132. Then in the third century AD, in an attack on Athens, the temple was wrecked and never repaired. We know the immense size of the temple from the platform on which the columns stood. The platform was 134.5 feet across and more than 350 feet in length. That's roughly the size of a football field.

CHAPTER 3
Better Than Perfect

At first glance, the Parthenon looks like a lot of other Greek temples from the same age. Like others, it is made of stone. But instead of limestone, much more expensive white marble was used everywhere. Even the roof tiles on the Parthenon were marble. (Roof tiles were usually made of clay.)

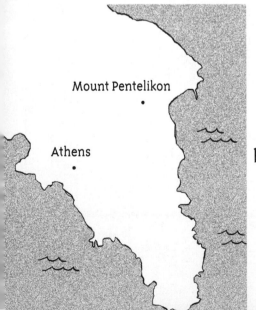

Mount Pentelikon

Athens

The marble for the Parthenon came from Mount Pentelikon, ten miles outside Athens. There, each block of stone was cut to the size and shape needed for its place on the temple.

The ancient Greeks had only simple tools, like hammers and mallets, to pound out the marble. Narrow grooves were hammered into the stone. Then wooden wedges were forced into the grooves. These wedges were soaked with water so that the wood would swell up and split off a piece of marble. Each piece was cut roughly into the shape needed for a particular spot on the temple: round pieces for the columns, blocks for the walls. Later on, at the Acropolis, the pieces would be polished and cut exactly to size.

None of the marble could have any cracks—it had to be perfect. The architects inspected every piece to make sure of that before it was carted to the Acropolis.

The heavy, rough pieces were carried to Athens on four-wheeled carts pulled by oxen; as many as thirty or forty pairs were needed for each! Mount Pentelikon was only ten miles away, but it was slow going to get to the Acropolis. It was usually a six-hour trip. Oxen could not make their way up the hill, so mules pulled the marble up the slopes of the Acropolis.

A marble floor for the temple was already there because years before, the people of Athens had begun building a different temple. Work had stopped when the Persians attacked. Having the floor already in place saved time and money for Pericles.

Building began with the construction of the forty-six outside columns. They would hold up the beams of the slanted roof. Each column was thirty feet high and made from round pieces of marble called *drums* that were stacked one on top of another. A square plug with a pin in the middle of each drum helped center it on the one below. Pulleys lifted up the drums—

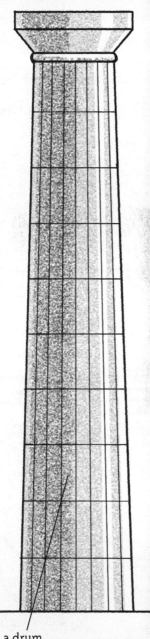

a drum

ten to twelve for each column. Winches and cranes were also used to put stone in place. Each drum had several *bosses*—big knobs—around which ropes were tied to pull the drum into place.

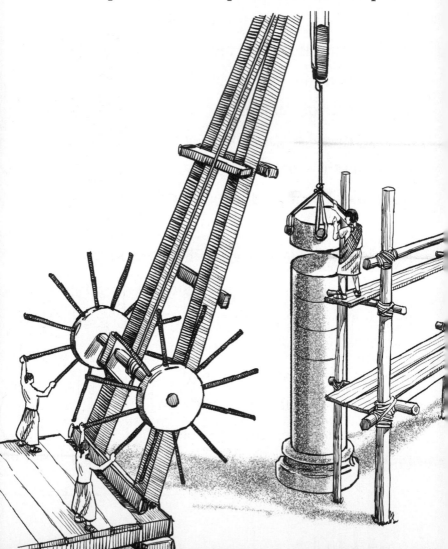

Once the columns were standing, skilled carvers hammered off the bosses and cut curved grooves all the way from top to bottom. This is called *fluting*. It looks a little like pleats in a skirt. There was no reason to do this except that it looked beautiful. Most of the column tops on the Parthenon are plain, but a few fancier ones have scroll designs. The plain ones are in a style called *Doric*. The fancier ones are called *Ionic*.

After the columns went up, work began on the two rooms inside the temple. In making stone walls, the blocks usually are held together with mortar. (Cement, for instance, is one kind of mortar.) But the blocks on the Parthenon fit

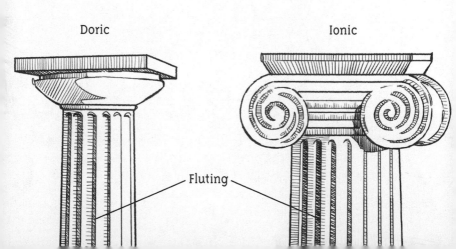

Doric

Ionic

Fluting

together perfectly. The space between them was nearly invisible. And no mortar was used. None at all. All that held the blocks together were metal clamps, which were hidden from view. They prevented the walls from moving.

The larger of the two rooms was to house the statue of Athena. The smaller was to store gifts that people would bring for the goddess: jewelry, gold, musical instruments, furniture.

The Parthenon follows the same basic design of many other ancient Greek temples. So what makes it stand out? Perhaps it will help to think of two cooks following the same recipe. They both use the same ingredients, but one of the meals will come out tasting much better than the other. Why? One cook changes the measurements of the ingredients a little. One cook experiments a little more and creates flavors that are simply more delicious.

For the Parthenon, little changes to the basic "recipe" for a temple make a big difference. Iktinos must have looked closely at many other Greek temples. And what he noticed made him change the design of the Parthenon in small but important ways.

For instance, temples with columns had always been built on perfectly flat bases. It seems logical to build this way. Yet the result was that these temples looked as if they sagged in the middle.

So the base of the Parthenon rises a little bit in the center. The effect of this building "trick" was to make the temple look lighter and balanced.

The Parthenon columns are different, too. Columns ordinarily were the same thickness from top to bottom. Like a pencil. Again, it seems logical. However, a row of perfectly even columns tended to look heavy and stumpy. The columns at the Parthenon taper slightly, like candles. They are thicker at the bottom than at the top. This small difference makes the columns appear more graceful.

Here are some other unusual facts about the columns:

The columns at the outer edges are fatter than the others.

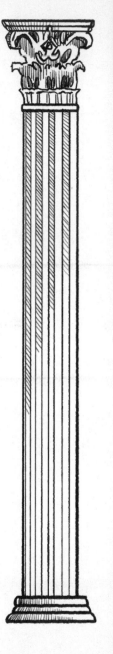

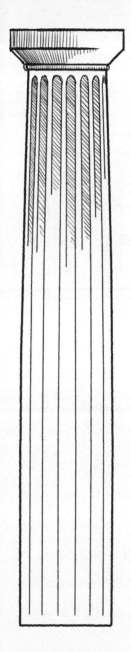

Every column bulges out slightly in the middle.

The columns do not stand perfectly straight. They lean in a little toward the middle. If the columns at either end could grow taller and taller, they would touch each other a mile into the sky!

Optical illusions are tricks that our eyes play on us. They make us see something differently from the way it really is. Iktinos understood optical illusions and used them in the design of the Parthenon. By purposely making things a little bit "off" or imperfect, Iktinos tricked people's eyes into seeing a temple that looked better than perfect.

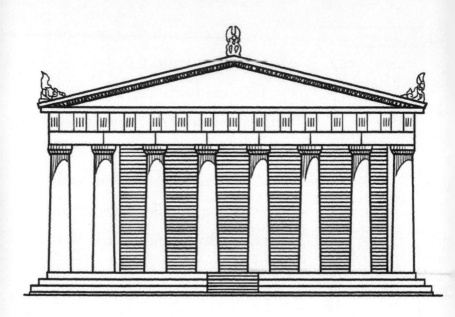

The Parthenon looks as if it is all straight lines, but the truth is that the temple is made almost entirely of gentle curves. The building appears as if every part of it is exactly where it should be. The temple is not too tall or too wide. The roof sits at just the right angle. Another way of saying this is that all the parts are in harmony. A famous French writer who saw the Parthenon said that it was

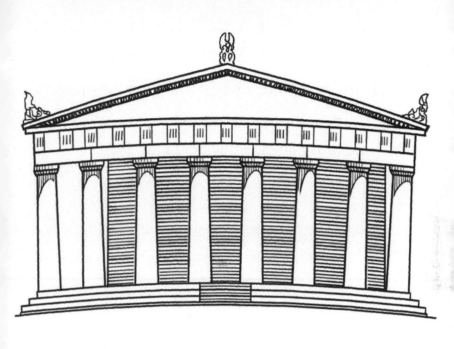

"the most perfect poem ever written in stone."
Other architects have described the Parthenon
as almost looking alive, as if the building were
breathing in and out.

But what made the Parthenon such a
spectacular work of art was not just the building
itself but all the statues and sculpture on it. No
other temple ever had nearly as much decoration.

Even though Pericles's enemies said the temple looked like an overdressed woman wearing too much makeup and jewelry, the general opinion is that the sculpture turned the temple of Athena into one of the greatest works of art ever.

CHAPTER 4
An Unusual Birthday

Pericles wanted statues and sculptures that would make the Parthenon "a source of everlasting fame." Phidias was the finest sculptor, so naturally Pericles turned to his friend to design the decoration on the Parthenon. Phidias did not personally carve most of it, but he planned how everything would look. It was his vision. And he personally created the showstopper—the forty-foot statue of Athena.

The sculptures on the temple appeared in three places. In bands called *metopes* (say: MEH-ta-pees) above the columns. In a frieze (say: FREEZE) all along the top of the inner walls. And in triangle-shaped spaces in front and back, made by the roof and support beams.

The triangular spaces are called *pediments*. They each housed about twenty-five larger-than-life statues. These statues were carved in studios near the temple and later lifted into place. Phidias probably designed them, but others did the carving.

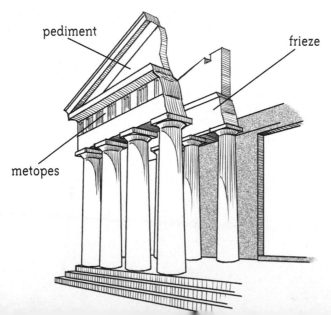

The pediments told the story of two myths that were important to the people of Athens. Less than half the pediment statues still exist. However, an artist named Jacques Carrey visited the Parthenon in 1674 and drew lovely, detailed pictures of the sculpture. That is how we know what much of it looked like.

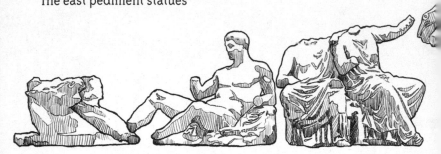

The east pediment is what people saw first when they walked up to the temple. On it was portrayed the story of the birth of Athena. She was Zeus's favorite child. And what a strange birth it was! Zeus, king of the gods, was suffering from a terrible headache. Finally, he asked another god to relieve his pain by splitting open his head with an ax. That certainly was an odd request. Yet the god had to obey his king, and when he struck Zeus, out popped Athena, fully grown and dressed, from her father's head.

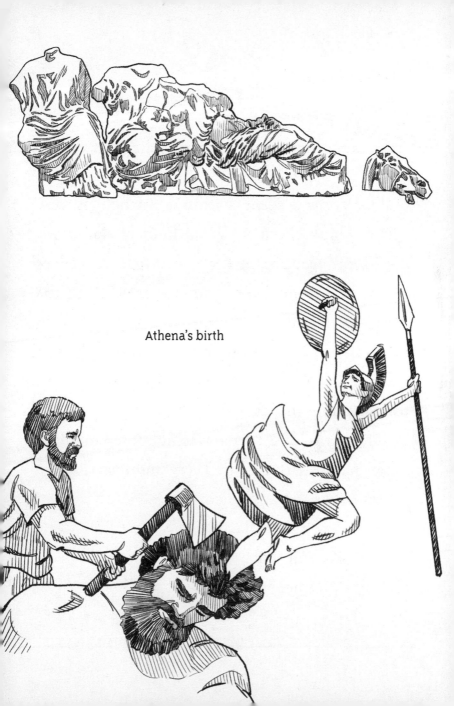

Athena's birth

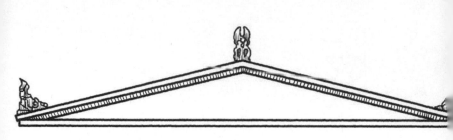

Depicting a scene within a triangle is very tricky. Think about it. What kind of statue can a sculptor place at either end where the edges meet at sharp angles? Little statues stuck in the corners would look silly next to ones that are so much larger. The sculptor of the group in the east pediment found a lovely, natural-looking way to use the oddly shaped space.

The birth of Athena was supposed to have taken place at dawn, the very moment the sun rises. So at one corner, it appears as if special horses (the sculptures are of only their heads) are rising up from the horizon to pull the chariot of the sun god. The other corner represents evening, the end of Athena's birthday. The tired horses of the moon goddess, having finished their long journey across the sky, are about to dip below the horizon. The design of the group represents the span of the day—sunup to sundown—on which the great Athena first appeared.

CHAPTER 5
A Grand Contest

The west pediment on the Parthenon portrays another myth of great importance: the contest to decide which god would become the special protector of Athens. The choice was between Athena and Poseidon, god of the sea. Each had to present an important gift to the city. Whoever gave the better gift would win the contest.

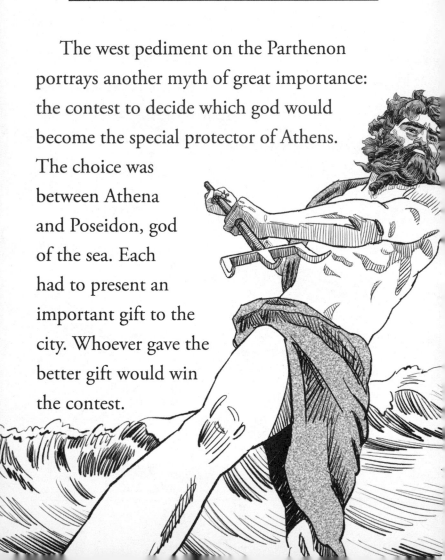

Poseidon struck his *trident*—a spear with three prongs—into the ground, and a spring of water gushed from the spot. Having water supplied to the city was certainly important. But Athena made a tree, an olive tree full of fruit, sprout beside the spring of water. Olive trees would produce food, as well as wood for building houses. So the twelve gods who were the judges declared her the winner. The city was named after Athena, and she became its protector. To this day, olives are a major crop in Greece.

Although we know which story the west pediment portrayed, many of the major statues in this group—both of Athena and Poseidon, for example—were destroyed, and no drawings were ever done to show what they had looked like. So archaeologists can take only a best guess at how the figures were posed and arranged.

Below the pediments are scenes carved into four-foot square panels of marble. These panels are called *metopes*. There are ninety-two of them. The figures—two or three on each—are carved quite deeply into the marble. But none of the figures are freestanding. They are attached to the marble block. Phidias hired many sculptors to carve the metopes that show battle scenes. And in all of the scenes, the Greeks are the winners. There are Greeks fighting centaurs—creatures that are half man, half horse. There are Greek gods wrestling with giants, and soldiers from Athens in battle with women warriors known as

Amazons. Only skilled sculptors were chosen to do the carving. Still, some were definitely more talented than others. In one metope, a centaur looks as if he has no neck!

The figures in the metopes were painted in various colors against a deep red background. In between the scenes were plain marble panels in deep blue. The bright colors helped make the scenes easier to see for viewers who stood far below on the ground.

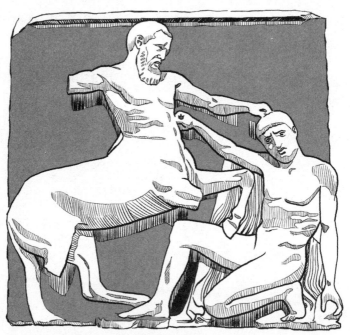

Great Heights

Why was all the sculpture on the Parthenon placed up so high? The pediments, the metopes, and the frieze were thirty-five to fifty feet above viewers' heads. One explanation is that it wasn't important whether ordinary people got a good look. The statues and sculpture were made for the goddess Athena, who could look down and view everything. The idea that the statues were made for the goddess may also explain why the pediment statues are carved in 3-D, although no one would ever see the back side of them. They had to be perfect all the way around because they were in honor of Athena.

CHAPTER 6
An Unsolved Mystery

Perhaps the strangest and most beautiful decoration on the Parthenon is the frieze. A *frieze* is a long strip of sculpture or painting on the wall of a building. At the Parthenon, a frieze runs all around the top of the inside rooms. The carving was probably done after the marble blocks were in place, with sculptors working on scaffolds.

The frieze was even harder to see than the statues on the pediments and the scenes on the metopes. That is because parts of it were hidden behind columns. Athenians looking in from outside caught only glimpses of the frieze. Yet, in many ways, it is the most amazing feature of all the artwork—and also the most mysterious. It is amazing because the frieze is 525 feet long— that's an awful lot of marble to carve. And it is mysterious because no one knows exactly what the frieze is showing.

Unlike the rest of the sculpture at the Parthenon, the frieze has suffered very little damage. It appears to be a procession or parade. More than six hundred figures are shown—about four hundred people and two hundred animals. There are girls carrying baskets on their heads and holding water jars. Boys pull cows and lambs along. People play musical instruments. Soldiers in armor ride horses or drive chariots.

The parade starts on one of the short walls, runs along both long side walls, and ends in the middle of the other short wall. The most important scene is there. It shows five figures that may be a family: a mother, father, and three children. On either side of the family, Athena and other gods sit and look on. One of the children is holding what appears to be a large piece of cloth.

For many years, it was thought that the frieze showed an important ceremony in Athens. Held every four years, it was called the All-Athens Festival. The whole city took part in the ceremony.

There were sports events, music contests, and even a male beauty pageant. However, the most important part of the festival was the parade.

Athenians wound their way up from the city to the hilltop temple of Athena. There, the goddess would be presented with a new robe.

Many historians believe that is what the child with the cloth is holding: Athena's new robe. Also, there are cows and lambs in the parade, which would be sacrificed for Athena. They were part of every All-Athens Festival.

Yet the idea that scenes showing a festival would appear on an important temple is odd. Temple sculpture portrayed important religious myths, like the birth of Athena, not holiday scenes. The parade

on the Parthenon frieze also contains other odd elements. There are things that don't appear in any other Greek artwork that shows the same festival. For instance, there are almost two hundred soldiers with horses on the frieze. They would not have been part of the festival; not in Pericles's day.

Recently, a book came out about the Parthenon frieze. It is written by Joan Breton Connelly, a well-respected archaeologist. An *archaeologist* is someone who studies very old objects to learn about what life was like in the past. Connelly is an expert on ancient Greece. In her book, she puts forth a very different idea about what the frieze shows. She thinks it is about a human sacrifice.

According to a very old myth, the first king of Athens was offered a deal by the gods. He was asked to *sacrifice*—put to death—the youngest of his three daughters. In exchange, Athens would remain safe from a powerful enemy. The king asked his wife what to do. What a terrible decision to make! Yet she agreed to the sacrifice. She thought it was better to let one person die, even if it was her own child, than to let all of Athens be destroyed.

According to Connelly, the five figures are the king, queen, and their three daughters. The person with the cloth is the daughter who will be sacrificed. Connelly believes she is not holding a new robe for Athena. The cloth is to wrap her own body in after she is killed!

This myth about Athens was a very important one. It was a *sacred*, or holy, story.

Connelly thinks that this legend fits in with the other stories portrayed in the Parthenon sculpture. However, there is no evidence to prove it for sure—or to disprove it. Phidias left no account of what the frieze was about. Neither did anyone else.

In the end, perhaps the exact meaning of the frieze is less important than how beautiful it is.

The carving is shallow—it has not been cut deeply into the stone. So the effect is more like looking at wonderful drawings in marble. The people appear real—that is, if real people looked perfect. There are so many small things to notice within the large crowd of parade-goers. A boy tries to coax along a cow who doesn't want to budge. An older man hobbles along on a stick.

Phidias himself is believed to have designed and perhaps sculpted the frieze. The carving is obviously the work of an expert, and he was the best of the best.

CHAPTER 7
Mighty Athena

The Parthenon had to be as big as it was in order to hold the giant eye-popping statue of Athena created by Phidias. Standing on a base, it rose to forty feet high. The outside, or shell, covered a hollow framework made from strong cypress wood. For the "skin" on Athena's face and arms, ivory was used. Ivory from elephant tusks that came all the way from Africa. Long, thin strips were cut from the tusks. Then they were boiled in beer until the ivory became soft enough to mold onto the statue. A pool of water in front of the statue kept the air moist and prevented the wood and ivory from drying out.

More than a ton of pure gold was hammered into thin sheets that formed the goddess's helmet, chest armor, robes, shield, and spear. Tiny nails held it all together. In her outstretched right hand was a six-foot statue of the goddess of victory. It was gold, too, as was a giant snake coiled next to Athena. (A real snake was also kept at the Acropolis to guard the sacred hill.)

The goddess statue alone cost more than the whole temple. And although many pieces of

Parthenon sculptures still exist, there is not a single trace of the giant Athena statue. At some later time in history, all the gold on it was removed and used to pay for the cost of wars. What happened to the rest of the giant goddess is a mystery. One guess is that a terrible fire in the third century AD destroyed all that was left of her.

So how do we know what the statue looked like?

Fortunately, way back in ancient times, many small copies of the statue were produced. They may have been made as souvenirs, like ones people buy today of the Statue of Liberty. In any case, that's how we know what the original looked like.

What Became of Phidias?

Although Phidias had a glorious career, he eventually ran into trouble. Athenians accused him of keeping gold that was meant for the statue of Athena. To prove his innocence, he took off all the gold and had it weighed. The weight was exactly the amount that Phidias had been given for the statue. Still, his critics did not leave him alone. Next he was accused of putting his own likeness and that of Pericles on the shield of the statue. That was a crime against the goddess! This time Phidias was found guilty. He was not allowed to remain in Athens and supposedly died in jail.

CHAPTER 8
The Parthenon and More

As splendid a sight as the finished Parthenon was, it did not stand alone on the Acropolis. Pericles was intent on building a whole complex— a group of buildings and temples that would show how powerful and important the city of Athens was.

In the years after the Parthenon was finished, a grand gateway was erected. Made of marble with columns on either side of the entrance, it blended perfectly with the style of the Parthenon.

To the side of the gateway is the Temple of Athena Nike. Yes, Nike just like the sneaker company. In Greek, *Nike* means "victory." Compared to the Parthenon, the small Temple of Athena Nike is almost like a child's playhouse temple—only eleven feet tall to the top of the pediment.

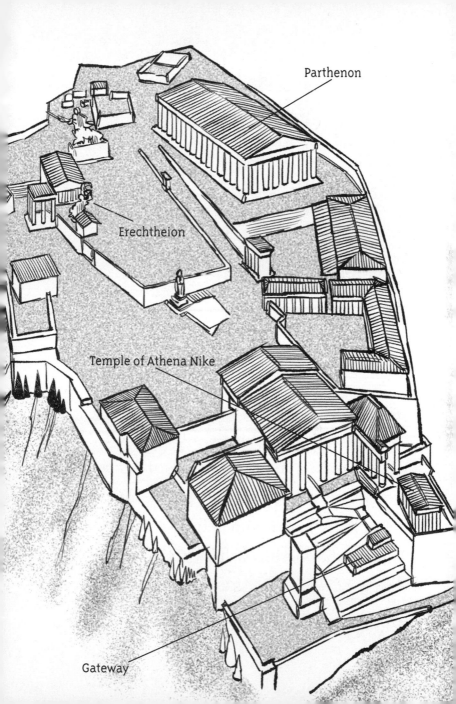

Parthenon

Erechtheion

Temple of Athena Nike

Gateway

Temple of
Athena Nike

Far more unusual is the Erechtheion (say: eh-REC-the-uhn), another temple to Athena. It sits across from the Parthenon on the other side of the hill. Its name comes from an early king of Athens who sacrificed his child. To the ancient Greeks, this temple was an even more sacred place than the Parthenon. Why?

It housed a wooden statue of the goddess made long before the Age of Pericles. It was this statue that was presented with the robe at the All-Athens festival.

The temple's most remarkable feature is the porch where, instead of columns, six marble maidens in long, flowing robes hold up the porch. They are called *karyatids* (say: carry-YAH-tids).

karyatids

Also in sight of the Erechtheion are traces from the contest for the city between Athena and Poseiden—the olive tree and the three marks from where the sea god's trident struck the ground.

Sadly, Pericles did not live to see the beautiful Erechtheion. A terrible sickness swept through Athens, killing a third of the people, including their leader. By this time, Athens was at war again but not with the Persians. The Athenians were now fighting other Greek city-states. It was a time of bloodshed and sickness and starvation. Athens's golden moment was over.

CHAPTER 9
In Ruins

After the Age of Pericles, Athens never again reached such heights of power and glory. Over the centuries, many different empires seized the area and took control of the Parthenon. There were fires—one in 195 BC, then a worse one between AD 200 and 300 in which the temple's roof collapsed.

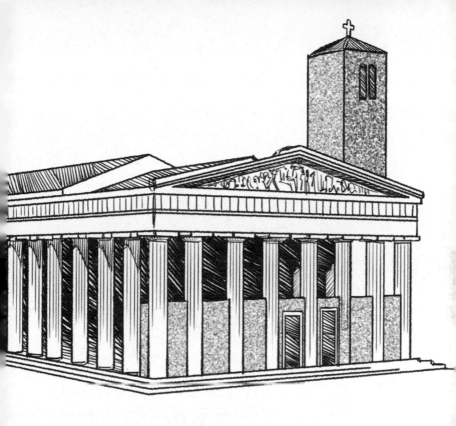

By the end of the AD 500s, the temple had become a church. First it was a Greek Orthodox church, then later a Roman Catholic church, with a bell tower added in the 1200s. Much of the sculpture was damaged on purpose because ancient Greek gods were not Christian.

In 1458, the Turks took control of Athens.

They followed the Muslim religion, so the Parthenon was turned into a mosque with a slender tower called a *minaret* attached to it. Even though the Parthenon was originally built as a temple to Athena, it served as a home to other religions for far longer.

By the end of the 1600s, the Parthenon was no longer used for any religious purpose. Instead the Turks now stored weapons and ammunition inside it. They were at war with the city of Venice, which is in Italy. The Venetians had the city of Athens surrounded. But the Turks didn't believe the enemy would ever attack the Parthenon—not such a world-famous landmark.

The Turks were wrong.

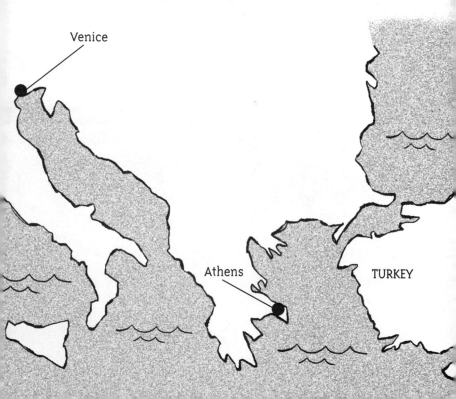

The darkest moment in the Parthenon's history came on September 28, 1687. The Venetian army fired seven hundred cannonballs at the Acropolis. One was a direct hit on the Parthenon. Three hundred people died. The temple's inner walls blew off, and many columns fell. Many sculptures were destroyed, including the ones on the west pediment showing the contest for Athens.

From that time on, the Parthenon was a ruin. It didn't even seem like a single building anymore;

it looked like pieces from two different buildings. One thing was certain: The Parthenon could no longer be used for any practical purpose.

Things only got worse. Local people would come and take pieces of marble to build new homes. Sometimes they heated the marble found on the ground in ovens until it turned into lime. (Lime was the main ingredient in cement.)

By the 1700s, there was interest in ancient Greece again. Tourists came to Athens from other parts of Europe, and even America, to study the history of the city and its monuments. Sometimes they took bits of the Parthenon home with them to keep as souvenirs.

The most famous "collector" was Lord Elgin of Great Britain. He was a nobleman who worked for England with the Turkish Empire. In 1801 he came to Athens, where the Turks were still in control. Elgin got a permit from them to take home marble. It is not clear from the permit exactly what he was allowed to take from the Parthenon. Elgin, it seems, believed the permit let him take pretty much whatever he wanted. It amounted to about half of the sculptures that had survived at the Acropolis.

Lord Elgin

Elgin paid what was then a fortune: about 35,000 pounds (in US dollars today, that would amount to $4.7 million). Between the years 1801 and 1811, he took statues from the pediments, most of the frieze, and several metopes.

Elgin shipped the artwork back to England and sold it in 1816 to the British government, which passed it on to the British Museum in London. That is where these pieces, known as the Elgin Marbles, are still exhibited. At first, not all museumgoers were impressed by the broken statues. They were in such terrible condition that Lord Byron, a famous poet, called them "misshapen monuments." But soon they became a huge tourist draw.

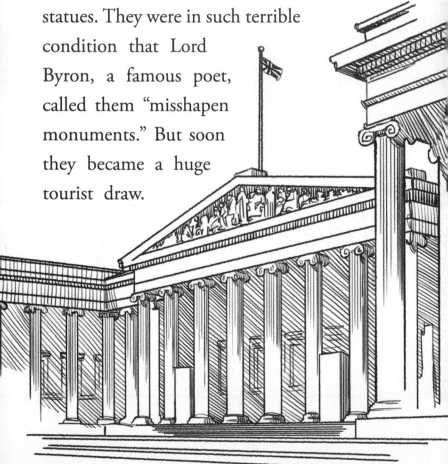

British Museum today

Today about 6.8 million visitors come to the British Museum, and hardly any leave without seeing the Elgin Marbles.

The people of Greece believe that Elgin stole priceless artwork that should be returned to its rightful home. By that, they mean their country. In England, the argument is that Elgin saved priceless artwork from being stolen or destroyed, and now that artwork can be enjoyed by everyone who visits the museum.

So what did Elgin do? Was it a robbery, a rescue effort, or a combination of both? The question of where the Elgin Marbles should reside is hotly argued. The sculptures have been in England for over two hundred years. They were in Greece for over two thousand years before that. More and more, museums that own artwork taken from another country are returning it. The Metropolitan Museum in New York City decided to give back a priceless Greek vase that had been found in Italy. It had been on exhibit for thirty-six years.

The larger question is really not about who owns what. The more important issue is to figure out how best to *preserve*—keep safe— what is left of the Parthenon and other temples at the Acropolis. They are buildings, so they stand outdoors. Unless at some point in the future an enclosure is built over the entire area, the Parthenon must weather through centuries more of sun, rain, and wind. And remember, the air today is much dirtier than it was even a hundred years ago. So every day, a little bit more of the Parthenon wears away.

After Elgin

Elgin was not the only "collector" of Parthenon sculpture. Some pieces have wound up in famous museums in France, Denmark, and other countries in Europe. As for the ones left on the Parthenon, they, too, reside in a museum now—a glorious museum in Athens that opened in 2009. The Acropolis Museum is

less than a quarter mile from the sacred hilltop with the temple. The sculptures are assembled in correct order around a rectangular area that is the same size as the "footprint" of the Parthenon. In the museum, however, all the sculpture is now at eye level, so visitors can see the incredible detail in the carving up close. And the museum walls are screens of glass, so visitors can look out and see the Parthenon itself while admiring the artwork made for it.

CHAPTER 10
The Parthenon Now

The Parthenon of today resembles the Parthenon of ancient times as closely as possible for something that is in ruins. Everything that was added to the temple over the centuries—the bell tower, the minaret—has been removed.

No parts of a Christian church or Muslim mosque remain. Nevertheless, work on the Parthenon still continues. Will new parts for what's missing be fit into the temple? Will copies of all the lost sculpture be put in place? Will the frieze and metopes be repainted?

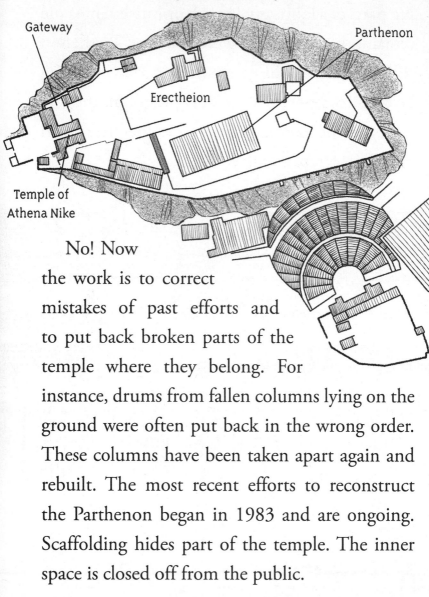

Diagram of the Acropolis

Gateway

Parthenon

Erectheion

Temple of
Athena Nike

No! Now the work is to correct mistakes of past efforts and to put back broken parts of the temple where they belong. For instance, drums from fallen columns lying on the ground were often put back in the wrong order. These columns have been taken apart again and rebuilt. The most recent efforts to reconstruct the Parthenon began in 1983 and are ongoing. Scaffolding hides part of the temple. The inner space is closed off from the public.

The new Acropolis Museum opened in 2009 and is a spectacular space exhibiting the sculptures from the Parthenon and Erechtheion that have remained in Greece. In great, airy halls, they are grouped as they originally appeared on the temples.

If people want to get an idea of what the Parthenon looked like when it was brand-new, they can travel to Nashville, Tennessee. There is a same-size replica, or copy, of the Parthenon in a city park.

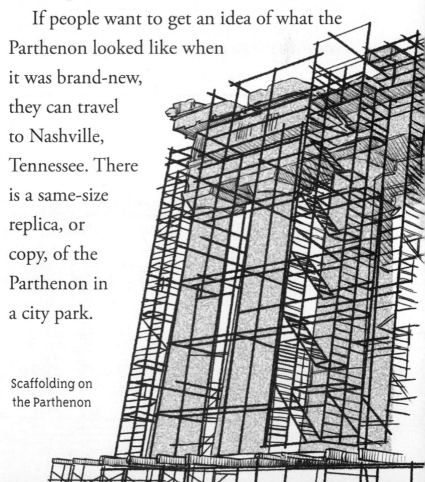

Scaffolding on the Parthenon

Why did Nashville decide to build it?

In 1897, a big fair was going to be held in Nashville to celebrate the state of Tennessee's one hundredth birthday. Because Nashville is sometimes called the "Athens of the South," the decision was made to build a new Parthenon in time for the fair.

Nashville's Parthenon includes copies of all the

sculpture. Inside there is even a full-scale statue of Athena with robes made of gold leaf. Instead of marble, though, the Nashville Parthenon is made of concrete. Concrete is a much cheaper building material than marble.

The temple in Nashville holds no religious ceremonies. Instead, it functions as a museum, drawing many tourists every year.

Parthenon in Nashville

Many other buildings around the United States are in the style of the Parthenon. Two famous ones are the US Treasury Building and the US Supreme Court Building, both in Washington, DC.

Supreme Court Building

They are proof that Pericles was absolutely right: What he was building was a monument for the ages. Athens's golden moment did not last long. Yet what remains of the Parthenon is still proof of the beauty that human beings, working at their very best, can create.

Pericles understood that. He said, in one of his most famous speeches to the people of Athens, "Our buildings and monuments command respect . . . In future generations men will marvel at us, as those who are alive today all marvel, too."

Timeline of the Parthenon

c. 5000 BC	People inhabit the area of the Acropolis
c. 500 BC	Greek city-states revolt against Persians for independence
c. 495 BC	Birth of Pericles
490 BC	Battle of Marathon with Athenian victory
480 BC	Persians capture the Acropolis, destroying many buildings
449 BC	War ends between Greeks and Persians, ushering in an age of peace
447 BC	Work begins on the Parthenon
432 BC	Work completes on the Parthenon
431 BC	War between Athens and Sparta begins again
429 BC	Death of Pericles
195 BC	A fire destroys part of the Parthenon
c. AD 200	In a second fire, the temple's roof collapses
c. 500	Christians convert the Parthenon into a church
1458	Parthenon is turned into a mosque
1674	Jacques Carrey sketches the Parthenon, including many of the sculptures
1687	Venetian army fires cannonballs at the Parthenon, setting off an explosion that turned it into a ruin
1801	Lord Elgin arrives in Athens and begins taking sculptures from the Parthenon
1983	Reconstruction efforts begin on the Parthenon
2009	New Acropolis Museum opens in Athens

Timeline of the World

Greek poet Homer writes *The Iliad*	c. 800 BC
Cleisthenes introduces Athenian democracy	507 BC
Philip II of Macedonia invades and conquers Athens, making it a part of his empire	338 BC
Construction begins on the first Great Wall of China	221 BC
Cleopatra becomes queen of Egypt	c. 51 BC
Construction of the Colosseum begins in Rome	c. AD 70
The fall of the ancient Roman Empire begins	190
Conflict between the Ottoman Empire and the Republic of Venice begins and lasts for more than eighty years	1423
Christopher Columbus sails to America	1492
The Taj Mahal in Agra, India, is finished	1643
Great Fire of London wipes out much of the city	1666
Declaration of Independence is signed; American colonies go to war against England	1776
The French Revolution begins	1789
War of Greek Independence from the Ottoman Empire	1821–32
Nashville celebrates one hundredth birthday, opening replica Parthenon	1897
World War I begins	1914
Greece joins the European Union	1981
Barack Obama takes office as the first African American president of the United States	2009

Bibliography

*Books for young readers

Connelly, Joan Breton. *The Parthenon Enigma.* New York: Random House, 2014.

*de Castro, Marisa. *The New Acropolis Museum: Monuments and Men. A Guide for Young People.* Athens: Metaichmio Editions, 2009.

Fagg, Christopher. *Ancient Greece* (Modern Knowledge Library). New York: The Warwick Press, 1978.

* Hynson, Colin. *How People Lived in Ancient Greece.* New York: The Rosen Publishing Group's PowerKids Press, Inc, 2009.

Macdonald, Fiona, and Mark Bergin. *A Greek Temple.* New York: Peter Bedrick Books, 1992.

Stuttard, David. *Parthenon: Power and Politics on the Acropolis.* London: The British Museum Press, 2013.